SCOTLA

GLASGOW

IN OLD PHOTOGRAPHS

GLASGOW

NIGEL DALZIEL

SUTTON PUBLISHING

Sutton Publishing Limited
Phoenix Mill · Thrupp · Stroud
Gloucestershire · GL5 2BU

First published 2002

This edition first published 2006

Reprinted 2006

Copyright © Nigel Dalziel, 2002

Frontispiece: Figures publicising the Glasgow
Bazaar of the Highland Association held in
St Andrew's Halls from 31 October to
2 November 1907. It aimed to promote Gaelic
arts, language and music and to encourage
the home industries of the Highlands and
Islands by selling their merchandise. Income
for the three days was £8,000.
Half title page: Evening Times paperboy, 1903.
Title page: The Glasgow General Warehouse
from before the First World War.

British Library Cataloguing in Publication Data
A catalogue record for this book is available from the
British Library.

ISBN 0-7509-4712-8

Typeset in 9.5/11 Photina.
Typesetting and origination by
Sutton Publishing Limited.
Printed and bound in England by
J.H. Haynes & Co. Ltd, Sparkford.

The Glasgow Soldiers' Home, 1914.

CONTENTS

The Royal Exchange, Queen Street, *c.* 1912. It forms the focus of the view westwards along Ingram Street and was originally built as the home of the extremely wealthy tobacco lord, William Cunninghame, in 1780. Later used as a bank, it then became the Royal Exchange after major reconstruction work between 1827 and 1832 during which it acquired this massive portico and a newsroom to the rear on what had formerly been the gardens of the house. The mansard roof storey was added in 1880 to accommodate the city's first telephone exchange. In 1949 the building was purchased by the corporation for £105,000 and subsequently housed Stirling's Library. It is now home to Glasgow's Gallery of Modern Art.

INTRODUCTION

As late as 1959 *Muirhead's Guide to Scotland* described Glasgow, Britain's third most populous city, as 'a busy, strenuous, and opulent commercial community and the centre of an industrial district, in which almost no manufacture in the United Kingdom is unrepresented'. But after 250 years, in which Glasgow built a remarkable prosperity based successively upon the transatlantic trade in the eighteenth century, then textiles, followed in the nineteenth century by iron, steel, shipbuilding and the manufacture of a comprehensive range of goods, the city's luck finally ran out.

The photographs in this volume belong largely to the early twentieth century, and they offer a glimpse of how much has changed within living memory. It was a period of civic pride and self-confidence seen not just in the great exhibitions in Kelvingrove, the royal visits to Glasgow and even in her frequently quoted soubriquet 'Second City of Empire', but in the straightforward achievements of the working man and woman whose labours supported the whole fantastical edifice. The Glasgow citizen had every right to be proud of shipbuilding most of all, the city's pre-eminent industry which grew largely on the basis of local talent, initiative and inventiveness, and was still producing half of all new world shipping tonnage in 1914.

The cost of this massive industrialisation and development, however, brought pollution, slums, misery, disease and an early grave to many of its people. As James Hamilton Muir (a composite name, incidentally, for three collaborative authors) commented in 1901, the West End mansions and the affluence of their owners were 'the silver lining of the clouds that hang over Govan'. Yet Glasgow was able to take an immense pride in its response to these problems through the agency of the Corporation which, in pioneering fashion, had set about the challenges of eradicating infectious disease, improving sanitation and providing decent housing by acquiring the necessary legal powers. A major agency in this process, the City Improvement Trust established in 1866, was years ahead of its time. Furthermore, the city's profitable tram system and utilities were widely praised. Glasgow was hailed as a super-efficient model municipality, and comparisons with the city-states of old fed its conceit. No wonder, in their satisfaction, large numbers of citizens failed to vote at election time, a trend still apparent today but perhaps, due more to dissatisfaction!

Although changing patterns of international trade, the decline of heavy industries and the pursuit of wholesale rebuilding schemes since the 1950s have had some terrible consequences for Glasgow, there is still a lot to admire. Much of its wonderfully rich architectural heritage remains and so does the resilient and resourceful Glasgow citizen, pioneering the way ahead for Britain's first post-industrial city. Let Glasgow flourish.

Nigel Dalziel
July 2002

LET GLASGOW FLOURISH

ARMS OF THE CITY OF GLASGOW

NEMO ME IMPVNE LACESSIT

1

East End

Nelson (later Albion) Street off Trongate, Glasgow, late nineteenth century.

Until the early nineteenth century Trongate was the principal street of Glasgow, its name derived from the public weighing machine (Tron) situated at the Tron Kirk. This building was the Town Hall, its grand assembly rooms the venue for important social events. Architecturally it was the most important building of eighteenth-century Glasgow, designed by Allan Dreghorn, built in 1737–40 and later extended. In 1780 it was bought by the Tontine Society which added an hotel at the rear with a coffee room below, accessed through the arches seen. The Coffee Room – the city's merchant exchange – was universally admired, the only dispute being whether it was the most elegant of its kind in Europe or just Britain. Here Glasgow's swaggering Tobacco Lords, the super-wealthy merchant elite, would daily hold court and tread the sheltered 'plainstanes' of Trongate in front, sweeping aside lesser mortals with their gold-headed canes. The building to the right with its distinctive steeple was the Tolbooth, or Town House, the hub of city administration, erected in the 1620s and given a new gothic facade in 1814 by David Hamilton.

Trongate looking east at the end of the nineteenth century. In the 1700s many of the buildings on Trongate had fine open arcades (inaccurately termed 'piazzas') on the ground floor, which gave the street a certain refinement and distinctiveness, and pedestrians some shelter from the weather. By the end of the century these had begun to disappear. The Tontine building is the last survivor in the late Victorian photograph, above, and was sadly demolished not long afterwards. The arches in the Tron Kirk steeple, below, seen in about 1904, were only inserted in 1855.

The corner of Trongate and Albion Street, *c.* 1911. The Tron Kirk was originally the Collegiate Church of St Mary, built in 1485, which apparently was accidentally burnt down by rakish members of the Hell Fire Club after a debauch on 8 February 1793. The wall on the left, at the corner of Chisholm Street, was built in 1900 to screen a railway tunnel air shaft. Below is Glasgow Cross, the old hub of the city, and the distinctive subway station, left, in about 1902.

Glasgow Cross was a congested crossroads at the junction of five main streets when the above photograph was taken in around 1914. Its surrounding buildings were also a mess. In that year a scheme was instigated to create an attractive sweep of new buildings with the rebuilt Tolbooth steeple at their heart. Permission to move the steeple was not forthcoming and it was left in place, right, when the rest of the Tolbooth was demolished in 1921. The traditional-looking Mercat Cross, with its raised platform and heraldic finial, dates from 1930 and was a replacement for one removed from the spot in 1659.

Mumford's Theatre building at the foot of Saltmarket, which runs from Glasgow Cross down to the Clyde. Mumford, who came from Bedfordshire, seems to have been a travelling showman and arrived in the city with a marionette show. From about 1835 this rough shack offered heavily melodramatic theatrical

performances, 'penny geggies', which provided popular working-class entertainment. A rival theatre owner managed to force its closure, but the shows continued under the redoubtable Mrs Mumford. By this date in the late nineteenth century John Cornin and E. Caldwell were in occupation selling second-hand clothes.

Close no. 139 off Saltmarket, 1880. Many of the
city's medieval buildings were destroyed in major
fires in the mid-seventeenth century, and this view
is typical of much of the later run-down and
overcrowded housing in this area of Glasgow.
The City Improvement Trust was created in 1866
to widen streets, demolish run-down buildings and
to reconstruct on a major scale.

Prince's Street off King Street, which led from
Trongate down to Bridgegate. This whole area was
'remodelled' in the late nineteenth century,
destroying the Tron Parish School, right. In about
1870 there were 87,000 children of school age in
Glasgow, yet two-fifths of them did not attend
school at all. This situation and the quality of
teaching radically improved following the passing
of the Education Act of 1872 and the creation of
the Glasgow School Board.

Gallowgate, which runs eastwards from Glasgow Cross through the district of Calton. It was the main gateway to the city from Edinburgh and the east and the location of the most celebrated Glasgow inn, the Saracen's Head at no. 203, roughly a quarter of a mile from the Cross. Here Samuel Johnson and James Boswell stayed on their return from the Hebrides in 1773; and William Wordsworth and his sister Dorothy *en route* to the Highlands in August 1803. Dorothy's journal describes her relief at being 'landed in a little quiet back parlour, for my head was beating with the noise of carts', and later, after a meal, 'walking a considerable time in the streets, which are perhaps as handsome as streets can be'.

Glasgow Cross looking up High Street, which was one of the four main streets of the medieval town. It led up to the Townhead area, the cluster of manses, fine houses and the Bishop's Castle gathered around the cathedral. High Street has suffered greatly from demolition, initially in the late 1700s, in order to improve access to the cathedral, and is now unrecognisable as an ancient thoroughfare.

Nos 17–27 High Street later in Victorian times. The working-class nature of the area is illustrated by these lodging houses for 'working men and travellers'. The arrangement of the gable-ends of buildings facing the street was a characteristic feature of old Glasgow, as were the ground-floor arcades originally stipulated by the town council. In about 1725 the much-travelled Daniel Defoe described the four principal streets, including High Street, as being 'the fairest for breadth and the finest built that I have ever seen in one city together. The houses are all of stone, and generally equal and uniform in height . . . ; the lower storey generally stands on vast, square Doric columns . . . and arches between give passage into the shops, adding to the strength as well as beauty of the building. In a word, 'tis the cleanest and beautifullest, and best built city in Britain, London excepted.'

Opposite: Old High Street looking south. The street developed strongly in the seventeenth and eighteenth centuries before industrialisation, decay and overcrowding set in and the heart of the city moved westwards. In the late nineteenth century the City Improvement Trust was responsible for demolishing much of the west side of the street and the slums behind.

Old Vennell off the High Street, 1888. The area was notoriously overcrowded and diseases, including cholera and typhoid, easily spread. From 1862 the city's pioneering Health Department began to get to grips with many of these problems. Wholesale demolition did the rest. Criminality was associated with slum conditions, and one Victorian commentator described the area as a magnet for 'the scum and the blackguards of the city'. Not a place for the fainthearted.

The Old College, founded in 1451 by Bishop William Turnbull, stood in the East End of Glasgow and occupied a suite of buildings begun in 1630. They were among the best examples of seventeenth-century architecture produced in Scotland. The East End was a poor and run-down area of the city by the early 1800s and many considered it an inappropriate site for a university. In 1863 the North British Railway Co. wanted the college site for a railway goods station and offered £100,000 for it. The university accepted, moved to Gilmorehill and tragically the Old College was razed.

The main entrance of the Old College on High Street showing the fine masoncraft which was an important element of the Scottish Renaissance architectural tradition. The carved panel above the entrance was completed in 1658, but when Charles II was restored in 1660 the royal arms were hastily added. Elements of the facade, dating from 1639, were saved and incorporated into Pearce Lodge at the new university site on Gilmorehill (see page 106). The entrance led through to two connected courtyards surrounded by the college rooms, a feature replicated at the new university site designed by George Gilbert Scott. The Old College was dominated by the large Dutch steeple.

The main entrance from High Street led
through an arcade into the Outer Court.
The Lion and Unicorn staircase ascended
to the Fore Hall, from which some
internal fittings were rescued and re-
installed in the new university senate
chamber at Gilmorehill. The staircase
itself, dating from 1690, was also saved
and re-erected against the west wing.
Further fine carved stonework, seen from
the stair, marked the entrance to the
Inner Court of the Old College, right.

Above the entrance arch into the Inner Court was the bust of the Reverend Zachary Boyd, graduate, a senior officer of the university over a long period, and minister of the Barony Kirk. He is best remembered for his long sermon attacking Oliver Cromwell, who was among the congregation, and his adherents on Sunday 27 October 1650. Boyd survived the encounter, although in return Cromwell invited him to a supper that was accompanied by a prayer of several hours duration, no doubt equally forthright, lasting until 3 a.m. When he died Boyd left a considerable sum to the university that helped pay for much of the new building, but on condition that two chambers were to be reserved for 'the chiefe man of the name of Boyd'.

The corner of Duke Street, left, and High Street showing the density of housing in the late nineteenth century. The social conditions were generally appalling in this part of the city and this was one of the reasons for the flight of the university to Gilmorehill. In 1853 Hugh MacDonald described the sin, misery and squalidness of the East End and its 'canopy of smoke' created by the mix of domestic fires and industrial workshops, breweries, dyeworks, mills as well as the railway locomotives arriving at the new College (later High Street) Station and the huge marshalling yards and goods station, which can be seen here upper left.

Duke Street, *c.* 1905, which is an eastward continuation of George Street. This new highway of 1794 was first suggested to the 'business-friendly' town council by the large and influential Carron Iron Co. of Falkirk as a more convenient route to and from the city by way of Cumbernauld. It was probably named after Frederick, Duke of York, although some say its name derives from the house of the Duke of Montrose situated near the junction with Drygate.

The retail sector grew considerably in the late 1800s helped by stable prices and increasing incomes. Slum clearance also helped by widening streets and creating more space for shops such as this, location and date unknown, selling lighting and household goods.

Glasgow Cathedral is a truly wonderful building dating from the late twelfth century although mainly of thirteenth-century design. It is dedicated to the patron saint of Glasgow, St Kentigern, known familiarly as St Mungo. He established a monastery here beside the Molendinar Burn from where he set about converting the Britons of Strathclyde. The chronicles suggest he died in AD 612. Because of the slope down to the burn, the eastern arm of the cathedral (on the right in this photograph) was built as a distinctive two-storey structure. The cathedral was substantially complete by the end of the thirteenth century, although the 220-foot central tower and other elements were finished during the 1400s. The final addition was the curious single-storey extension from the centre of the building (south transept) known as the Blackadder Aisle or Chapel, built by Archbishop Blackadder (died 1508), possibly above the grave of St Fergus. Thankfully, after the Reformation in 1560, the burghers of Glasgow adapted the cathedral for the new forms of worship which helped to preserve it from the destructive zeal of the reformers. Three separate congregations came to occupy different parts of the building. In the foreground is James Hamilton's graceful Bridge of Sighs (1833–4) with a single 60-foot span taking the road over the now-culverted Molendinar Burn to the Necropolis. Immediately to the left of the cathedral is the Royal Infirmary.

The nave, the western arm of the cathedral, above, was built during the late thirteenth century, but its completion was possibly delayed well into the fourteenth century due to the War of Independence with England. Bishop Robert Wishart (1271–1316) was even accused of using timber earmarked for its construction to make siege engines. The building is relatively small (319 feet long by only 63 feet wide) but appears larger due to its height, narrowness, simplicity of the carving, and the massing of the columns and arches. The steps and a door in the fine carved fourteenth-century rood screen lead up to the choir, below looking west, completed under Bishop Bondington (1233–58).

The twelfth-century crypt, or Laigh Kirk (Lower Church), is one of the most impressive and sophisticated medieval vaulted structures in existence. It was extended by Bishop Bondington in the thirteenth century and housed the tomb of St Mungo, centre, of which only the base remains. It was an important centre of pilgrimage. From 1595 until about 1798 it was the home of the Barony Kirk, then partly filled with earth and used as a burial ground until it was thankfully restored, with the rest of the building, in the nineteenth century.

The vestry has housed a number of interesting items associated with the history of the cathedral, including Cromwell's chair, said to have been used by the Lord Protector during his visit to the city in 1650.

View towards the west end of Glasgow Cathedral, above, showing very clearly the massed tombs and monuments of the Necropolis, a commercial venture laid out from 1833 by John Bryce on the Fir Park. It was the third 'hygienic cemetery' in Britain and was modelled on Père Lachaise in Paris. After 1835 there was a commendable and successful system of vetting 'to prevent the construction of monuments in very bad taste'. Surmounting the whole is the Doric column crowned with a statue of John Knox erected in 1825. Below is the cathedral around 1930 with a statue of James White of Overtoun, city benefactor, erected in 1891.

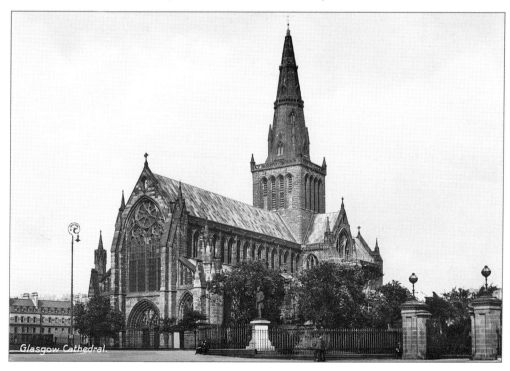

Glasgow Cathedral.

Provand's Lordship on Castle Street was built in 1471 and, apart from the cathedral, is the only pre-Reformation building left in Glasgow. It was the manse for an adjoining Hospital of St Nicholas and later the town house for the Prebend of Barlanark, or Provan. It is the only one of many medieval buildings near the cathedral to have survived the nineteenth-century clearances. This engraving is dated 1853 and shows the small, low cottage to the left which was the home of the Glasgow hangman.

In 1906 the Provand's Lordship Society acquired and restored the historic building. In 1927 the great Glasgow shipping magnate Sir William Burrell helped the society to furnish the house in the style of about 1700. Contents included Scottish oak furniture and four Flemish tapestries, as here in the 'Mary Queen of Scots bedroom' which she supposedly occupied during a visit to her lover Darnley in 1567.

The People's Palace on Glasgow Green was opened on 22 January 1898 by the Earl of Rosebery for the cultural benefit of the population of the deprived East End of the city. At the opening ceremony Baillie Bilsland referred to its 'combination, practically under one roof, of a museum, picture gallery, winter gardens and music hall' as being possibly unique in Great Britain. It has been the city's cherished museum of local history since the 1940s.

Templeton's Carpet Factory beside the Green is one of Glasgow's architectural gems. The firm's directors commissioned William Leiper to design the factory in Venetian style. It was completed in 1889 and is known as the Doge's Palace. The building's extravagant design incorporates coloured bricks and tiles as well as stone dressings. It was converted for use as a Business Centre in 1984.

William Stark won the competition to design the new courthouse, municipal offices and gaol to succeed the old, cramped Tollbooth. It was built between 1809 and 1814 in the austere Greek Revival style, one of the first and finest examples in Britain. The height of the surrounding roads was raised when Hutcheson Bridge was built between 1829 and 1834, giving the building a sunken appearance. This photograph shows it after its conversion in 1910–13 solely for court use.

Glasgow Corporation began supplying electricity in 1892 and by 1914 there were 50,000 domestic consumers. Industrial demand also increased and the Corporation opened new power stations, including this one at Dalmarnock in 1920. It was taken over by the British Electricity Authority in 1948. (*Glasgow Corporation Electricity Department, courtesy of Scottish Power*)

2

Central Glasgow

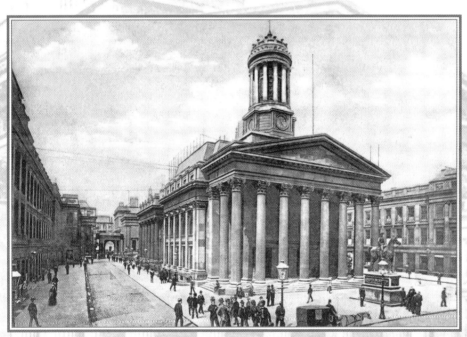

The Royal Exchange and statue of the Duke of Wellington, *c.* 1900.

Argyle Street developed westwards from Trongate in the eighteenth century. Although this photograph from the early 1900s shows the street looking fairly quiet, it was part of the main business district which was normally thronged with shoppers, visitors, businessmen, clerks, street vendors, idlers and a cross-section of city life that spelled Glasgow to many people.

John Anderson's Royal Polytechnic Warehouse on Argyle Street was, in fact, the city's first department store established in 1845 (Hugh Fraser's Buchanan Street store was founded in 1849). It became Lewis's, whose building dates from only 1932, but is still familiarly known as the Poly. At the turn of the nineteenth century the building boasted this tremendous Byzantine-style smoking room for refreshment and relaxation.

Two views of Argyle Street from the Heilan'man's Umbrella, the bridge which carries the railway across the road into Central station, at the crossing of Union Street, left, and Jamaica Street. One of the standard tramcars, introduced in 1898, is on the route between the city and the exhibition, held at Kelvingrove in 1901. On fine evenings it was a different place, full of young working-class lads and lassies promenading and courting, and on Saturday night a place of drink, fights and excess before Sunday brought peace and calm once again. Such was its split personality.

Views of Argyle Street looking west from the St Enoch Square corner towards Central Station, the shop awnings all in use on the sunny northern side of the street. In the centre is the prominent department store which is now Fraser's. Below, in this view from the 1920s, signs advertise all manner of shops and goods, including Gerber Brothers & Co., 'wholesale jewellers and watch factors', left, and nearby the St Enoch Picture House, one of Glasgow's popular early cinemas.

Busy Buchanan Street, above, at the corner of Argyle Street in the early 1900s, was the home of many highly regarded and prestigious retailers. The large store here belonged to R. Stewart, described in the *Post Office Directory* as 'goldsmith, watchmaker, turret-clock maker and, by appointment, silversmith to the Queen'. Below, the street in the 1920s as motor cars began their slow rise to ascendancy over the horse and carriage.

Buchanan Street, 1920s. Among the business signs is 'Cranston's Tea Rooms' at no. 28. The tea room as an institution was an offshoot of the temperance movement and was pioneered in Glasgow by Stuart Cranston who opened the family's first premises in 1875. Stuart's sister, Kate Cranston, exploited its potential by opening her own establishment in Argyle Street in 1878. Other branches followed, including this entire building in Buchanan Street in 1897. Tea rooms were increasingly popular, offering

respectable ladies comfortable alcohol-free premises (as well as lavatories, vital on long shopping expeditions to the city) and dining rooms. There were even smoking and billiard rooms for the men with whom they were equally popular. Kate Cranston is widely appreciated for her patronage of rising artistic talents George Walton, Charles Rennie Mackintosh and his wife Margaret, practitioners of the 'Glasgow Style', who were responsible for much of their fittings and decoration.

Buchanan Street was named after Andrew Buchanan. The maltster became rich on the sale of American tobacco and owned a house and land here. It was first feued in 1777, although he sold the property soon afterwards when the American War of Independence led his companies into bankruptcy. The street was intended for the mansions of the wealthy, but became one of Glasgow's premier shopping streets which, according to the *Glasgow Herald* in 1903, had 'always been reckoned the finest thoroughfare in the city'. Despite the rivalry of upstarts such as Sauchiehall Street, it still retains its position as Glasgow's most fashionable shopping street. In contrast to this view taken around 1930, the street is now pedestrianised.

The 9 a.m. Glasgow–Perth express train headed by the Caledonian Railway locomotive no. 14448 at the company's Buchanan Street Station, some time after 1912. The terminus was opened in 1849 and closed in 1966.

The visit of the new king, Edward VII, and Queen Alexandra, to Glasgow on 14 May 1903 was an occasion of unmitigated popular rejoicing. Even the itinerary and route of the royal procession were keenly anticipated and the papers sold well on the story. The *Evening Times* reported it on 24 April along with the ordinary everyday fare which included 'Housebreaking in Glasgow – lady's plucky action'.

King Edward and Queen Alexandra stayed overnight at Dalkeith Palace and arrived at Queen Street station in Glasgow the following day, 14 May 1903, at noon. They had lunch in the City Chambers in George Square and afterwards were driven to the Kelvingrove art galleries and the university by way of Buchanan Street, seen here. The *Glasgow Herald* reported that 'thousands of the proletariat flocked to the central thoroughfares' to see the king and queen, and Buchanan Street which, 'clad in all the plenitude of its decoration, resembled a fairy avenue'.

The city's new double-decker electric tramcars (500 were introduced between 1898 and 1902) were also part of the celebrations. The *Glasgow Herald* reported that at dusk on the eve of the royal visit, 'the Corporation ran a number of illuminated cars over the principal routes, and their progress called forth loud cheering'.

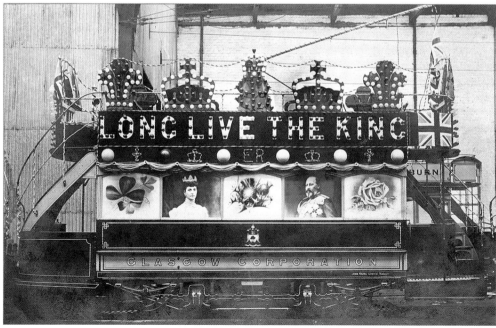

On 23 April 1907 Glasgow welcomed the Prince and Princess of Wales (the future George V and Queen Mary) during an extended visit to the district, during which they were awarded the Freedom of the City and honorary degrees at Glasgow University. The prince also unveiled a memorial stone to his grandmother, Queen Victoria, at the Royal Infirmary at the start of major rebuilding works.

Another royal visit, another illuminated tram. Between 8 p.m. and midnight on the eve of the prince and princess's visit these Corporation tramcars trundled about town and were particularly noticeable on level streets such as the Great Western Road where they could be seen at a distance. According to the *Glasgow Herald*, 'each carried a band discoursing patriotic and popular airs'.

Union Street, laid out in 1815, extends northwards from Argyle Street and leads into Renfield Street. This is a scene from the mid-1920s, complete with tram to Shieldhall and the bustle associated with the central shopping area and entrance to Central Station on the left.

The Adelphi Hotel at the corner of Union Street and Argyle Street in 1935. To the left at 14–22 Union Street is Shaw Walker Ltd, ironmongers and manufacturers of 'patent Sine Qua Non kitchen ranges', who also sold home furnishings, kitchen and household utensils, glass and enamelware and at this time advertised the 'lowest prices in the city'. (*Library of the University of St Andrews*)

Gordon Street has many fine Victorian commercial buildings and Glasgow's major Central Station. From here the Caledonian Railway provided services to and from the Clyde Coast, south-west Scotland and England. It opened in 1879 and superseded the company's Buchanan Street Station, which thereafter concentrated on services to the north and north-east.

The original intention was to surround the station with the company's headquarters, but instead it built an hotel to better the impressive St Enoch Station Hotel nearby which belonged to the rival Glasgow & South Western Railway Co. The Central Station Hotel, seen here, was designed in a neo-Queen Anne style and completed in 1884.

The atmospheric Central Station concourse. Above the ticket office, centre, was the 73-feet-wide set of train information windows serviced by a nimble group of staff who raced to keep up with the rapid number of arrivals and departures. It was converted to a restaurant in the 1980s and computerised indicator boards were sensibly introduced.

This photograph shows something of the capacity and character of the building in the early 1900s. Its expansion to thirteen platforms took place between 1899 and 1906, superintended by the Caledonian's chief engineer, Donald A. Matheson, whose streamlined concourse was full of curves and rounded corners – quite an advance.

Renfield Street, which runs north from Hope Street, *c*. 1904. The sign advertises B. Anderson, tobacconists, possibly the firm based at 24 George Square and owned by William Murray Bruce.

The North British Railway Hotel in George Square was associated with the adjoining Queen Street Station which can be seen to the left of the building, above. It occupied early nineteenth-century premises which were converted in 1903–5 with the addition of the extra storey and attic. The photograph opposite, above, shows its earlier appearance. It became the Copthorne Hotel in 1986. George Square's position, close to the central shopping and business areas that developed with the westward expansion of the city, made it a favourite location for hotels from the early nineteenth century onwards.

The entrance to Queen Street Station, 1902. It is the oldest of Glasgow's stations and began life in 1842 as the western terminus of the Edinburgh & Glasgow Railway. Its most striking feature is the massive half-moon roof of 1878–80 designed by railway engineer James Carsewell.

The Glasgow Division of the Corps of Commissionaires, 1904. Reception and security duties at hotels and other buildings were taken very seriously by this uniformed body of men, many of them former soldiers. In 1901 the organisation's 'commander' was Parr Campbell of 68 West Regent Street.

Glasgow's City Chambers in George Square, designed by William Young of Paisley, are among the most opulent in the country and perfectly demonstrate Glasgow's wealth and importance in the late nineteenth century. Construction began in 1883 and the building was officially opened by Queen Victoria in 1888. Late eighteenth-century plans for a grand residential square with Adam-designed buildings were never realised. It became a commercial area, encouraged by the intrusion of the railway station, and then the civic centre of Glasgow with plenty of statuary in honour of the great and good.

On the third floor of the building is the rather sombre Council Chamber, above, designed for the seventy-five city councillors. The Lord Provost's chair was Queen Victoria's gift to the Corporation at the opening. The building's interiors took until 1890 to complete due to their elaborate design which incorporated rich woods and many other opulent materials, including particularly fine Italian marbles used in the fireplaces. Electric lighting was installed from the start.

The Cenotaph, George Square, was designed by Sir J.J. Burnet and dedicated by Earl Haig of Bemerside in 1924. As Sir Douglas Haig, the Commander-in-Chief of the British Armies in France (and a fellow Scot), he was given the Freedom of Glasgow on 8 May 1919.

During his visit to Glasgow on 14 May 1903 King Edward VII laid a foundation stone for the new technical college buildings on George Street. This temporary platform, with canvas roof lined in cream and gold, was erected to accommodate the official party. Glasgow was *en fête* despite the poor weather and according to an unusually purple-pencilled *Herald* reporter, 'we were privileged to bask in the radiance of royalty'.

The Glasgow and West of Scotland Technical College had its origins in the Andersonian Institution – originally termed 'university' – established through the bequest of John Anderson (1726–96), Professor of Natural Philosophy (physics) at the University of Glasgow. His interest was in the practical application of science to industry and in the education of working-class 'mechanics'. These principles continued to guide the governors of the college, who in 1886, saw their remit as affording 'a suitable education to those who wished to qualify themselves for following an industrial profession or trade'. This photograph shows the impressive Royal College building on George Street designed by David Barclay and completed in 1905.

The college's architecture was described in 1903 as being a 'free treatment of Italian Renaissance design', which also created some handsome stairways! The two-acre George Street site, the accommodation on five floors and semi-basement and the number of students made the technical college the largest in Britain. The final cost of the land purchase and building construction was £210,000.

The Hydraulics Department was one of seventeen departments of the tech installed in the Royal College building in 1905. Here are some of the demonstration weirs and turbines used for teaching and experimentation.

The library of the new technical college, which was given a good start to its collection of books and publications through the bequest of John Anderson's own personal library. The demand for learning was huge and the college flourished, helped by amalgamations with other institutions along the way. It was also responsible for administering Allan Glen's School. In 1903 the college had 596 day students and 4,394 who attended evening classes, all taught by around 80 members of staff. In 1903 the *Glasgow Herald* recorded that its students could be found throughout the world 'holding important positions as mechanical and electrical engineers, railway and harbour constructors, manufacturing chemists, mine managers and metallurgists and the like, while practically every large industrial establishment in the Clyde area numbers past students among the members of its respective staff'. It became the University of Strathclyde in 1964.

The 100-ton metal-testing machine in the Mechanics Laboratory, above, part of the Practical Engineering Department. Below is the Motor and Dynamo Laboratory in the Electrical Engineering Department. Together with the Hydraulics Department they were situated at the bottom of the interior courtyards of the new building, lit from the roof, and occupied around 30,000 square feet of floor space.

The Botany Laboratory, part of the Biology Department, with its impressive natural history teaching collection tastefully arranged for the photograph. Below, the Dyeing and Printing Laboratory, two skills long practised in the Glasgow area in the textiles and book and newspaper publishing industries.

Furnace Room, Metallurgy Department. Other departments of the college included bakery, chemistry, mechanics, machine design, mining and geology, architecture and building construction, reflecting the range of skills taught by the college and giving an idea of the diversity of the Glasgow economy at that time.

St Vincent Place, the eastern arm of St Vincent Street looking towards George Square, just before the First World War. It dates from 1804 and is lined with handsome commercial buildings, particularly banks and the former Anchor Line offices at nos 12–16.

The wide and impressive St Vincent Street, *c*. 1903. It was extended westwards from St Vincent Place in 1809; the name commemorates the great British naval victory over the French and Spanish in 1797. It was intended as a residential street, but was colonised by business from the mid-nineteenth century. Perhaps the best of its architectural highlights is Alexander 'Greek' Thomson's St Vincent Street Church, the powerful temple designed in a fusion of Classical and Egyptian styles, which dominates the hill.

Striking west from Hope Street is Bothwell Street. It was originally residential, although after the entrepreneur James Scott got his hands on the area after 1849 the street was widened, joined to St Vincent Street and became heavily commercialised. The Christian Institute and YMCA, centre, were built between 1878 and 1896 but have not survived the passage of time. They were replaced by an undistinguished office block (100 Bothwell Street) in 1987.

On 17 August 1909, as the *Glasgow Herald* reported, 'one of the most extensive and disastrous fires that has occurred in Glasgow for several years broke out shortly after midnight in Ingram Street within 30 yards of the Central Fire Brigade premises'. It caused damage estimated at a massive £250,000 affecting many properties and at least twenty commercial tenants who held large, flammable stocks of goods.

The blaze was first noticed by a duty fireman at the station at 12.21 a.m., but it spread from the top floor to envelop the whole four-storey building in fifteen minutes. Firemen could do little to bring it under control and had to dodge back into the fire station when the stone façade of the top storey crashed into the street at 1 a.m. They were then forced to turn their hoses on their own station which was imperilled by the intense heat.

As the fire spread eastwards the fire brigade, including colleagues brought from all the district stations, succeeded in saving Hugh Buchanan's wine and spirit shop at the corner of Shuttle Street and also College Home, a model lodging house on High Street which provided accommodation for between 300–400 men. Around 1.30 a.m. its occupants were forced to evacuate the building, the firemen's hoses being used to encourage some of the laggardly occupants. They were allowed to return between 4 and 5 a.m. What started the fire never became clear but it led to many workers being made redundant, including girls employed in Harris & Dietrichson's ladies' underwear workshops.

3

Southwards
& the Riverside

The paddle-steamer *Eagle III* (1910) leaving the Broomielaw, probably on the 11 a.m. run to Rothesay, early in the 1920s.

Jamaica Street Bridge, also known as Glasgow Bridge or Broomielaw Bridge, *c.* 1903. Below, one of the busy 'cluthas', river ferries, can be seen embarking at the Broomielaw. Behind the right-hand bridge lamp-post is the Glasgow Custom House, on Clyde Street, which James Hamilton Muir described in 1901 as 'a solemn little thing . . . placed in an out-of-the-way corner which only highly-trained civil servants can readily find'.

A wonderful view of the Jamaica Street Bridge busy with traffic, including Ibrox and Linthouse trams. Jamaica Street itself, extending from Argyle Street down to the river, was put through in 1761–3 as part of the city's westward expansion and development, the name reflecting the city's strong trading links with the West Indies. The old Glasgow Bridge upstream was inadequate, so Jamaica Street Bridge was opened as a second crossing in 1772, although this was later demolished and replaced in 1833–6 by a bridge designed by the great Scottish civil engineer Thomas Telford (1757–1834). Even this bridge proved inadequate for the volume of traffic and it required strengthening against the river; so by popular demand a larger replica of Telford's bridge was built and opened in 1899 re-using much of his original stonework. To the left of the Jamaica Street Bridge is the Central Station railway viaduct of 1876–8 built for the Caledonian Railway Co. which demolished an insalubrious area west of Jamaica Street to make way for Central Station. The company added a second bridge immediately downstream between 1899 and 1905 when the station was enlarged.

The bridge in the 1920s leading across to the city proper, when motor buses were becoming a common sight for both transport around the city and for excursions to the country. Visible across the river are the premises of Paisley's Ltd, clothiers, at 82–96 Jamaica Street.

St Enoch Square, the site of the main Glasgow & South Western Railway Station (1876), with its 204-foot-wide roof, and hotel (1880) seen here in the early 1900s. In the foreground is the pretty little Jacobean-style former underground railway ticket office of 1896. It is also visible in the picture at the top of the opposite page.

The name of the square is derived from St Thenew, the mother of St Mungo, and it was planned as a select residential area in 1768. It became simply the open space in front of the railway station, complete with taxi rank and cabmen's shelter. The station and hotel were sadly demolished in 1977 to make way for the St Enoch shopping centre and its even vaster station-style glass roof.

The Broomielaw from the Sailors' Home, looking upstream, at the end of the nineteenth century. This was the harbour of Glasgow from medieval times, associated with the city's illustrious history of maritime trade and particularly with pleasure trips down the Clyde on steamers such as the ones shown above. The quay and its landing sheds closed in 1947.

King George V Bridge was opened in 1928 beside the Central Station Bridge of 1899–1905 which was itself built directly alongside the existing railway bridge of 1878. The new road crossing connected Commerce Street, above, with Oswald Street on the north side of the river. It is a concrete bridge pretending to be a traditional-looking three-arched granite bridge, but none the worse for that. In 1934 the Clyde Navigation Trust, whose domed building can be seen below, left, insisted on maintaining headroom of 18½ feet above high water to allow vessels access to the quaysides upstream. (*Lower picture: Library of the University of St Andrews*)

A typical scene at the Broomielaw in the early years of the twentieth century, where travellers, holidaymakers and even commuters gathered for journeys to and from the growing towns and villages along the Clyde Coast and the islands. The demand for shorter journeys led to intense competition among the various steamer operators who continually acquired faster vessels; and among steamer captains – never shy retiring types – who were sometimes prepared to be extremely reckless with their ships and the lives of their passengers for the honour of being first to arrive in port. To achieve this result stops were even missed out *en route*. Efforts by the River-Bailie Court, which fined and banned the worst offenders, caused this to cease in the 1860s, but rivalry remained intense.

A view of the Broomielaw in the early 1900s, including the Clyde Navigation Trust (free) ferry, left, plying between West Street, by the Kingston Dock, and York Street. Since the 1840s the trust had also operated a fleet of ferries, distinct from the cross-river services, known as 'cluthas', one of which can be seen right. A ticket for their 3½-mile run between Victoria Bridge and Whiteinch cost 1*d*.

MAGNIFICIENT NEW

Pleasure Sailing   on th

had a splendid day on

The Clyde passenger steamer *Queen Alexandra* shortly after she was launched in 1902. She was built by Denny's at Dumbarton for Turbine Steamers Ltd of 99 Great Clyde Street, Glasgow, managed by John Williamson, a talented steamer captain, qualified engineer and partner in the company. The new technology of turbine propulsion gave her a speed approaching 22 knots, which was much

BINE STEAMERS IRTH of CLYDE.

QUEEN ALEXANDRA

on Board
S.S. Queen Alexandra
Campbeltown
July 03
splendid
steamer this
we have
and. Regards to all
Lyle

appreciated on her long voyages between Campbeltown and Glasgow. This regular run continued until 1911 when she caught fire, and was then sold to the Canadian Pacific Railway Co., which changed her name to *Princess Patricia* and employed her on services out of Vancouver, British Columbia. She was scrapped in 1937.

The Clyde was home to many famous shipping companies, notably the British India Steam Navigation Co. whose operations were focused on eastern waters. It was founded in 1856 by (later Sir) William Mackinnon and his early partner Robert Mackenzie, both from Campbeltown. Mackinnon began his working life in the Glasgow office of a Portuguese East India merchant, and by 1881 the firm owned and managed 70 ships. BI ships were registered in Glasgow and the Clyde shipyards built most of the company's fleet. Although the *Morvada*, above, was built on Tyneside, her sister ship *Merkara*, below, was built by Connell's at Scotstoun, both in 1914, the year BI amalgamated with P&O. In 1922 the fleet numbered 158 ships, the largest in the world.

The river wharves and anchorages were usually full of shipping, here including the Dublin-registered *Saint Kevin*. There had always been an active trade with Ireland. Early in his career the Glasgow grocer Thomas Lipton collected goods from vessels arriving in the river and later went to Ireland himself to buy hams and other provisions direct. The massive expansion of shipping trade and traffic in the nineteenth century led to the building of new docks leading off the river. The first was Kingston Dock, opened in 1867, followed in 1880 by the Queen's Dock, which had a water area of 34 acres and is seen below in 1915.

Thomas Lipton, who founded his chain of grocery shops in 1871, is probably the most famous retailer to have emerged from Glasgow. His success was based on cheap and direct selling using inspired advertising campaigns represented by this photograph, publicising his own-brand tea produced on his plantations in Ceylon from the 1880s. His firm came to hold royal warrants for the supply of provisions to the royal family.

The Prince and Princess of Wales (later George V and Queen Mary) being driven through Glasgow during their visit in April 1907. One of the prince's engagements was to open the Rothesay Dock, built by the Clyde Navigation Trust which had taken over the role of managing the river from Glasgow Corporation in 1840. Its main tasks were to improve the Clyde for shipping and provide all the appropriate infrastructure for ships to load and unload goods. The growing number of ships, their increasing size and the need for more space led to a huge investment in docks which were built further down the river. Between 1897 and 1907 this helped the trust to increase its revenue from £400,000 to £530,000 a year in a trade that seemed to have no limits.

The Rothesay Dock at Clydebank, newly opened by the Prince of Wales on 26 April 1907 and built to handle coal exports and imports of ore and other industrial commodities. It was designed for ease of railway operation and was one of the first docks in Britain operated solely by electricity.

Prince's Dock at Cessnock on the south side of the river was opened in 1897 to handle general cargo. It was the largest dock in the estate of the Clyde Navigation Trust and frequently full to capacity. This view, taken in the 1920s, shows its continuing importance. It closed in the 1970s, however, and was the site of the 1988 Glasgow Garden Festival.

The River Clyde at Scotstoun facing upriver with the tug *Flying Meteor* towing the Ellerman Line's *City of Singapore*, built at the Alexander Stephen yard, Linthouse, 1951. Glasgow had led the way in marine technology and manufacture from the early years of the nineteenth century, recognised in 1812 when Henry Bell's *Comet* became the first commercially successful steam vessel. Shipbuilding was encouraged by

CITY SINGAPORE

a flourishing iron and steel industry up to the First World War and the activities of the Clyde Navigation Trust in deepening the river this far upstream. Steel and shipbuilding became the foundations of the Glasgow economy. By this time, however, and for many reasons, shipbuilding was in severe decline, an economic and often personal loss that no one has been able to remedy. (*Ralston Series postcard*)

The fitting-out basin at Fairfield's yard, Govan, and the heavy-lift crane which was the largest in the world when it was erected in 1911. The shipyard, seen here in 1911 or 1912, had been set up in 1861 by Randolph, Elder & Co. at Old Govan, but in 1864 the company bought the larger Fairfield site after which the yard was named. John Elder (1824–69) was one of the most eminent and talented engineers of the day, inventing the much more economical compound engine which allowed steamships to conquer the world. Other technical innovations kept the yard at the forefront of shipbuilding. By 1870 it employed 4,000 men and was the largest private shipyard in the world, producing large fast liners, cargo vessels and, as here, warships for the Royal Navy. It survived until 1968 when it was absorbed into Upper Clyde Shipbuilders, now Kvaerner Govan.

The entrance to Fairfield's yard at Govan, *c*. 1905. These were busy years for the yard and for Clydeside generally, the annual production of ships along the river rising from 50,000 tons in 1859 to 757,000 tons by 1914, half the world total. The industry employed 100,000 men directly and in associated trades.

Water Row, beside the Govan Ferry, *c*. 1905. This picturesque row of traditional cottages was noted by James Hamilton Muir in 1901 as 'the last remnant of the old salmon-fishing village of Govan . . . high and dry above the ferry conduit [foreground]. Time was when the . . . ferryman who lived here pushed his way between a fleet of fishers' cobbles'.

Govan's Town Hall of 1901 is a large and magnificent building which suitably reflected its importance as the fifth largest police burgh in Scotland (it had a population of 91,000) and an impressive industrial growth based on shipbuilding and engineering. It was incorporated into the City of Glasgow in 1912.

The Elder Free Public Library on Langlands Road, Govan, was opened in 1903. The money for this building and its fine book collection was provided by Isabella Elder, widow of John Elder of Fairfield's shipyard. Figures of a shipwright and draughtsman form part of the Govan coat of arms on the central balustrade.

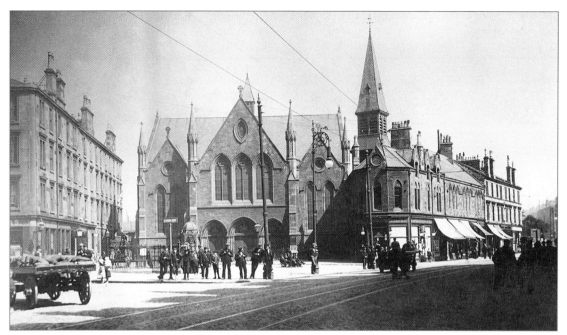

Govan Cross, with its irregular open space, *c.* 1913. This is still the hub of Govan town centre even in its rebuilt state. It formerly served as an open-air forum where the burning social and political issues of the day were debated, particularly in the 1930s. In the centre of this photograph is Govan Old Church, built as St Mary Govan Free Church in 1873.

Govanhill only became established in the 1870s following the sale of land for development by the proprietor of the local Govan Iron Works, William Dixon Smith. The new burgh of mainly working-class tenements required the usual facilities, and this photograph from about 1908 shows the Holy Cross Chapel and school. It was the first Catholic church in Govanhill.

Many municipal parks were developed from the mid-nineteenth century largely for the health and welfare of the urban population. Glasgow had opened sixteen by the time of the First World War. Queen's Park was created out of the Pathhead Farm lands comprising 143 acres and although it was outside the city boundaries it catered for the growing population south of the river. It was formally opened in September 1862 and commemorated Mary Queen of Scots who was defeated at the Battle of Langside (1568) to the south of the park. The Camphill estate was added in 1894.

Elphinstone Tower, Gorbals in the late nineteenth century. Across the river from Glasgow, at the southern end of the original medieval Glasgow bridge, is the district of Gorbals, originally a small village with surrounding lands which belonged to the Bishops of Glasgow. After the Reformation the property was acquired by Sir George Elphinstone, a wealthy merchant and Provost of Glasgow, who built a fine new mansion off Main (now Gorbals) Street to which this tower was later added. After Glasgow Town Council bought the estate in the mid-1600s the mansion was occupied by its baillie, the official who administered the burgh until it was absorbed within the boundaries of the City of Glasgow in 1846. The former mansion was used as the burgh courthouse, police post and lock-up as well as school and assembly room. By then the area had become industrialised and overcrowded, much of the housing degenerating into slums. Elphinstone mansion suffered the same fate and it was demolished in 1866.

The solidly working class Oatlands area of Gorbals, south of nearby Richmond Park, included Rosebery Street, above, and Logan Street, seen below at the corner of Wolseley Street, in the early 1900s. The Railway Mission Hall at 19 Logan Street was a common feature of such areas. So were dairies supplying fresh milk: Hamilton's dairy was situated in the row next to the mission hall and at 91 Rosebery Street.

4

Westwards

A delivery boy at Kelvin Bridge, Great Western Road,
in the early 1900s.

Two views of Sauchiehall Street in the early 1900s. The photograph above shows the junction of West Campbell Street looking east. On the left is Rodmure's, which operated a school of cookery, laundry and housekeeping and a school of dressmaking, millinery and underclothing under a manager, Mr J. Fox, and Lady Superintendent Mrs Fox, known as Madame Levine.

Bright and lively Sauchiehall Street looking west at the junction of Hope Street, *c.* 1903. The Anniesland tram was one of many that slowly rumbled up and down all day. Sauchiehall became a prime location in the central shopping and commercial district which stretched for 2 miles from Glasgow Cross to Charing Cross, and is perhaps Glasgow's best-known street for both shops and entertainment. On the right of the photograph at no. 116 is the shop of P. & P. Campbell, dyers and cleaners; and above at no. 118, the surgery of dentist Donald R. Cameron, who commuted to work daily from Newlands Road, Langside. According to J.H. Muir, in 1901, the area to the right of this view, 'from the little squalid lanes round the theatres down to the bright pubs and shady supper rooms of Sauchiehall Street . . . is the Soho of Glasgow'.

Above: Sauchiehall Street, *c.* 1908, at Cambridge Street looking east and terminating at the junction with Parliamentary Road. *Below*: looking west from the Renfield Street crossing in about 1930 with Bruce's Furniture Galleries on the corner.

The 198-bedroom Beresford Hotel in Sauchiehall Street was opened on 28 April 1938 and built to coincide with the British Empire Exhibition which attracted millions of visitors to Bellahouston Park. Bed and breakfast cost 12*s* 6*d*. The fashionable concrete building was designed by James W. Weddell and William Beresford Inglis, a Glasgow cinema owner, and its façade included three vertical fins decorated with mustard, black and red faience. The coming of war undermined its profitability and Beresford was ruined. It is now the University of Strathclyde's Baird Hall.

Glasgow Boys' High School on Elmbank Street, in the early 1900s. It originated in the medieval cathedral school which was later taken over by the Town Council. It became increasingly selective and parted company with the city education authorities in 1976 when it amalgamated with Drewsteignton School and moved to a new site at Old Bearsden.

Kelvinside Academy, Bellshaugh Road, a select boys' schools that opened in 1878 with the development of the west end of the city. It is satisfying to note that Garnethill Public School, opened the same year and situated in a lower-middle-class district, recruited more successfully than the rival Kelvinside Academy and the Glasgow Academy, which moved to Kelvin Bridge in 1878.

The King's Theatre on Bath Street was designed by the famous theatre architect Frank Matcham and was built between 1901 and 1904. It seated 2,000 and became the city's premier venue for touring companies. It took a long time for the dour Calvinist community of Glasgow to reconcile themselves to theatrical entertainment. In 1764 a permanent theatre was set up on the site of the current Central Station, although on the opening night the complete interior, including props, costumes and scenery, was destroyed by arson. All was soon restored and the theatre continued until it burned down completely in 1782, a fate which befell a large number of the city's playhouses at one time or another. According to Cleland's *Annals of Glasgow*, the spectators cried 'save the ither folks' hooses an' let the De'il's hoose burn'. Many other theatres followed, however, especially after licensing restrictions were removed in the 1840s. The King's Theatre became the first home of the Scottish Opera in 1962 and is still operated by Glasgow City Council.

The actor (later Sir) John Martin Harvey (1863–1944) as Hamlet, who performed the title role at the King's Theatre. The theatre attracted many distinguished performers and Harvey was a world-famous romantic actor highly acclaimed for his Shakespearean roles in which he toured the provinces.

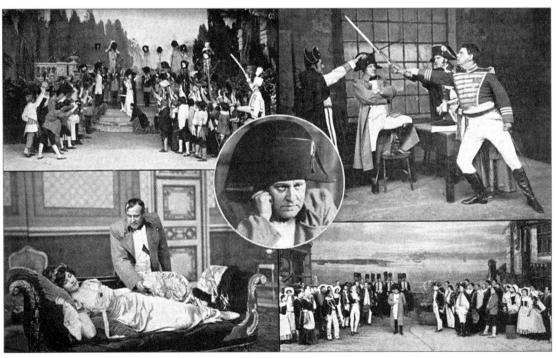

The Theatre Royal in Hope Street, originally the Royal Colosseum, was considered the most prestigious theatre in Glasgow and among its many offerings was, in November 1915, *A Royal Divorce – A Story of Waterloo*. It was performed by a London company and starred Juan Bonaparte, apparently the great-grandson of Napoleon I.

More's Hotel, India Street, which first appeared in the *Post Office Directory* for 1911–12 with Miss Jessie M. More as proprietrix. This area of the city was completely redeveloped in the 1960s and '70s, destroying the attractive terraces of houses which the hotel occupied. Penguin's *Buildings of Scotland – Glasgow*, describes it now as 'a bureaucratic backwater', the home of Customs & Excise, Inland Revenue and various council offices, all in 1970s brick.

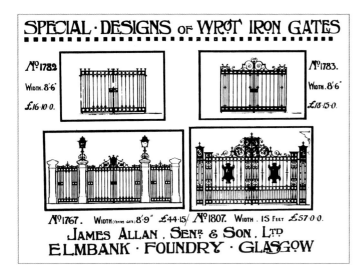

The ornamental ironwork seen in India Street was something of a Glasgow speciality, the most famous producer being Walter Macfarlane's Saracen Foundry, Possilpark. There were many others, including James Allan's Elmbank Foundry at 12 Possil Road, described as 'ornamental and sanitary ironfounders' in the 1900–1 *Post Office Directory*. Their products graced many city streets until the Second World War and were exported widely overseas.

St Columba's Gaelic Church on St Vincent Street, with its distinctive 200-foot spire, is so large and magnificent that it is sometimes described as the 'Gaelic Cathedral'. It was built between 1902 and 1904 using the compensation paid by the Caledonian Railway Co. which had demolished the Hope Street Church to make way for Central Station.

St Andrew's Halls of 1873–7 were celebrated for their role in the musical cultural life of Glasgow and for the finest acoustics of any concert venue in Britain. Tragically, they were gutted by fire in 1962 as a result of a discarded fag-end left after a boxing match. Only bits of the structure remain. The site now houses the Mitchell Theatre and the extended Mitchell Library, another great Glasgow institution.

The face of Charing Cross, 1903, all but destroyed by the intrusion of the M8 ring-road completed in 1980. On the left of the no. 905 Kelvingrove tram is the Grand Hotel, managed by Mr C. Ulbrich, which was a casualty of the destruction. It was regarded as the smartest hotel in Glasgow at the time.

Charing Cross again, the gateway to the West End from Sauchiehall Street and the city. The Grand Hotel is on the left and ahead is the distinctive curve of Charing Cross Mansions, a fanciful French Second Empire-style design by Sir J.J. Burnet. It is still with us but the original plate-glass shop windows on the ground floor have been spoiled and are now much less elegant than in this picture from the 1920s.

Woodside Red Cross Hospital, Park Drive, was completed in 1915 as the Glasgow College of Domestic Science. Because of wartime requirements the Scottish Branch of the Red Cross was permitted to convert the building to a 330-bed auxiliary hospital formally opened on 29 June 1915 by Lord Provost Dunlop.

A characteristic feature of the Park skyline, overlooking Kelvingrove, is the group of four tall towers. Three belonged to Trinity College, seen here, formerly the Free Church College of 1856–61, now converted to flats. The fourth, on the right of this photograph, is the only surviving part of the parish church of 1858 which was demolished in 1969.

The long, straight Great Western Road heading out of the city towards the West Highlands is perhaps the most impressive boulevard in the country. An Act of Parliament in 1836 permitted the making of a turnpike road from St George's Cross to Anniesland Toll and the many attractive terraces and villas which grew up on the adjoining estate lands of Woodlands, Hillhead and Kelvinside soon satisfied the demand for better-class housing. These photographs were taken in about 1905 looking across the Great Western Bridge of 1890–1 which spans the 182 feet of the River Kelvin on two cast-iron arches. Above, a Dennistoun tram heads east towards the city passing the Caledonian Mansions of 1897 at the corner of Otago Street, right. The slender 218-foot spire of Lansdowne Church dominates both views, with the spire of St Mary's Episcopal Cathedral beyond.

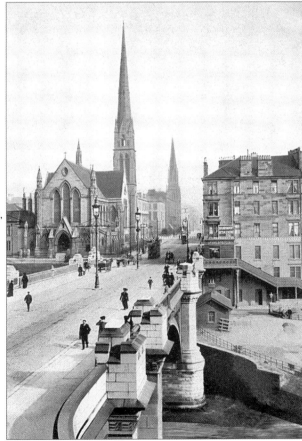

The entrance to the Botanic Gardens, opposite Grosvenor Terrace, before and after the electric tramcars were introduced in 1901. Behind the entrance, at the junction with Queen Margaret Drive, are two half-timbered pavilions of 1894, put up at the same time as the old Botanic Gardens Station with its distinctive gilded onion domes. It was demolished in 1970. In 1901 James Hamilton Muir described the Great Western Road as 'the pride of Kelvinside, and, until the cyclists laid it waste it deserved its praise'!

Carnarvon Street in the Woodlands area west of today's M8, full of attractive terraces and tenements developed from the early years of the nineteenth century. The wealthier lived up on nearby Woodlands Hill and in the crescents from where the menfolk commuted into the city or to their respective places of work. James Hamilton Muir commented, in 1901, on the resulting 'nearly deserted streets, which, but for ladies and children, would be entirely lifeless . . . [with] . . . here and there a school for young ladies or for instruction in art'. Perhaps this photograph shows one of them, right, with the name 'St George's Art . . .' above a window full of framed paintings.

The Botanic Gardens, seen here in about 1907, have their origin in the Physic Garden of the University of Glasgow on High Street which gradually moved out of the city to this larger 22-acre site between the Great Western Road and the River Kelvin. The Royal Botanic Society of Glasgow opened it to the public in 1842, but the gardens were taken over by the Corporation and opened as a public park in 1891, later enlarged to 44 acres. The pleasant walks and range of glasshouses became great favourites, not least with the nursemaids and their charges from the well-to-do houses nearby.

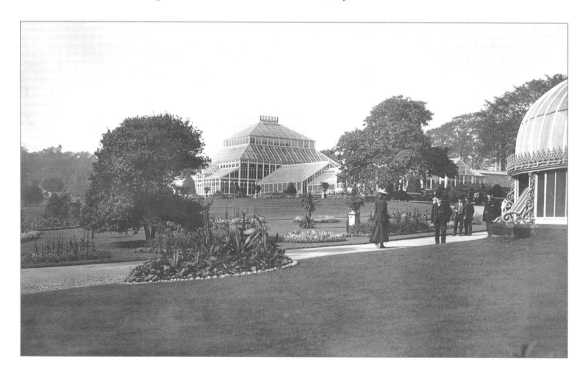

The best known glasshouse is the Kibble Palace, below right, named after John Kibble, a wealthy businessman, engineer and amateur inventor, who had the giant conservatory built at his house at Coulport, Loch Long, in 1863–6. It was re-erected in the Botanical Gardens in 1871 as the Kibble Crystal Art Palace and Royal Conservatory with an enlarged 146-foot central dome. The meeting and concert venue was operated by Kibble himself. It is said to have accommodated over 4,000 people on the occasion of William Gladstone's speech here in 1873 following his installation as Lord Rector of Glasgow University.

The Kibble Palace also incorporated a smaller 60-foot diameter dome near the main entrance, seen here in about 1910. It was described as the Fern House and was connected to the main dome by a long passageway. The humidity, exotic lush foliage and erotic sculptures may explain its popularity and Kibble's lease turned out to be very profitable until the society decided to buy him out and return the building to its original function as a glasshouse in 1881, precipitating its own bankruptcy and Corporation control.

Queen Margaret College, on Queen Margaret Drive, *c.* 1906. Northpark House had been built in 1869 for wealthy art collectors, but in 1883 it was bought as the home for the first Scottish higher education institution for women. In 1895 John Keppie and Charles Rennie Mackintosh collaborated to design the rear extension which was used by Glasgow's first female medical students. In 1935 it became the headquarters of the BBC in Scotland.

Kelvinside bowling green with the college to the right.

Queen Margaret Bridge, which only dates from 1926–9, carries Queen Margaret Drive past the old
Queen Margaret College and across the River Kelvin on a 135-feet wide concrete arch. The roadway
between the parapets is a generous 80 feet wide.

Byres Road, leading from Partick, was the main street of Hillhead which became a police burgh in 1869
with a population of 7,738. It developed strongly in the mid-nineteenth century as a residential area,
which it largely remains, but its independent existence came to an end in 1891 when it was absorbed
by the city of Glasgow.

5

Kelvingrove

Spinning wool beside the Cross of Iona in the
Highland Clachan, Scottish National Exhibition,
Kelvingrove, 1911.

The entrance to Kelvingrove Park, *c.* 1905, with Glasgow University dominating the scene. On the left lay Kelvingrove House, begun in about 1783 for Lord Provost Patrick Colquhoun. It was demolished in 1901 although the 1876 extension, seen here, was left standing and used as the Japanese Pavilion in the 1901 Exhibition. Colquhoun was the most prominent of the fabulously wealthy Glasgow merchants trading with America and was the founder of the city's Chamber of Commerce, the first in Britain.

Pearce Lodge, completed in 1888, forms the gatehouse entrance to Glasgow University off University Avenue. Thanks to the generosity of Sir William Pearce, a prominent engineer and shipbuilder, architectural elements of the demolished seventeenth-century Old College were saved and re-used in the gatehouse. They including the main rusticated arch, heraldic panel and window heads. Behind is Sir J.J. Burnet's Engineering Building of 1901.

Music in the park, *c.* 1908. The university buildings were fairly new at this time following the move from Glasgow's run-down East End. The Gilmorehill site, seen here, had been the property of various West India merchants and, from 1845, the Glasgow Western Cemetery Co. which had intended to build a necropolis, but in 1865 it was bought for £65,000 for the new university buildings which were erected in the twenty years from 1866. The architect was Sir George Gilbert Scott, the English designer of, among other things, the Foreign Office in London, who was a great proponent of the Gothic Revival style. His appointment was not well received in Glasgow, not least by Alexander 'Greek' Thomson, Glasgow's own architectural genius whose designs would have been much more striking.

There have been many eminent members of staff and graduates of Glasgow University: Adam Smith, who held the Chairs of Logic and of Moral Philosophy from 1751 to 1763, and William Thomson, Lord Kelvin (1824–1907), foremost among them. This is a study of Lord Kelvin, Professor of Natural Philosophy at Glasgow for fifty years and the greatest physicist of his day whose interests spanned many areas of science. He was particularly interested in electrodynamics and was responsible for technical advances which led to the successful laying of the Atlantic submarine telegraph cables in 1866. He had an international reputation, was naturally honoured with the Freedom of the City of Glasgow, and was one of the first recipients of the Order of Merit – a fitting tribute.

Glasgow Corporation bought the Kelvingrove estate in 1852 for a public park and in 1870 the mansion was opened as an industrial museum. Its exhibits included this early beam engine, designed by James Watt, who was born in Greenock in 1736 and initially employed as a mathematical instrument maker at Glasgow University. He went on to become the world's greatest mechanical engineer whose development of efficient steam engines can be said to mark the start of the Industrial Revolution.

The magnificent centrepiece of Kelvingrove Park is the Stewart Fountain, erected in 1871/2 to commemorate Lord Provost Stewart, who was responsible for supplying the city with clean, fresh water from Loch Katrine. The fountain was restored in 1988.

In typical Victorian fashion, Kelvingrove Park is full of statues, and this view shows the unlikely representation of a Bengal tigress bringing a peacock to her cub. It is situated below the fine houses of Park Terrace. The statue was the gift of John S. Kennedy of New York, to his native city of Glasgow in 1867.

Close to the Prince of Wales Bridge is the memorial to the Highland Light Infantry, a Glasgow regiment. It commemorates those who fell in the Boer War in South Africa (1899–1902). It was a popular war which generated widespread excitement, shown here at the official unveiling in 1906. The statue was the work of Birnie Rhind.

The Prince of Wales Bridge in Kelvingrove Park is a beautiful, classical single-arched bridge of red sandstone, 40 feet wide. It was erected in 1894/5 to the design of the City Engineer Alexander B. McDonald. It crossed the River Kelvin below Woodlands Hill, seen here crowned with the grand sweep of Park Terrace, right, and Park Quadrant, left. These fine attractive terraces, perhaps the best in Glasgow, were built in 1855–8 after plans fell through to relocate Glasgow University to the site. They represent the finest work by architect Charles Wilson, who was responsible for encouraging the corporation to buy Kelvingrove Park in 1852. Although Sir Joseph Paxton, architect of the Crystal Palace at the Great Exhibition, London, in 1851, submitted a plan for Kelvingrove three years later, work had already started on the 'pleasure grounds' and it is probable that Wilson, with surveyor Thomas Kyle, was chiefly responsible for the layout of the park and its network of features and wooded walks.

Glasgow University looking down on the Kelvin some time before the First World War. In the foreground is the trestle bridge built for Glasgow's second exhibition in 1901 which (as in the 1888 Exhibition) even saw an authentic Venetian gondola (and gondoliers) gracing its waters. To the right, and below, are the Kiosk Tea Rooms which were built as Van Houten's Cocoa Kiosk for the 1901 Exhibition, one of the many refreshment buildings located throughout the park.

The Rockery Bandstand, near the Kiosk refreshment rooms and Kelvingrove Art Gallery to the left. Below is perhaps a hint of why the park was so popular in days of old. There were always plenty of stories of romantic liaisons associated with the exhibitions in the park. Courting couples were especially fond of rides in the amusements sections and anywhere on the walks where the lights were absent.

Kelvin Way Bridge, *c.* 1929, built between 1913 and 1914 to take the new road through Kelvingrove Park, viewed from the Art Gallery. On the right are the popular bowling greens created after the 1901 Exhibition and on the other side of Kelvin Way are some later bowling greens and tennis courts surrounding the pavilion of 1924.

The Kelvin Hall had its origins in the 1901 Kelvingrove Exhibition Machinery Hall, and when it burned down in 1926 the city engineer, Thomas Somers, designed this replacement exhibition venue. It was the largest of its kind in Britain, with 170,000 square feet of floor space, which was ideally suited to its role in the Second World War as the country's main factory producing convoy and barrage balloons.

Above: The Grand Concert Hall looking towards the Industrial Hall, the main building of the International Exhibition at Kelvingrove in 1901. The event was intended to display the progress of nineteenth-century industry, science and art, but music was an essential part of making it a popular success. The concert hall seated 3,000 and was in daily use. However, some thought the musical fare very lacklustre despite a budget of £20,000, mostly spent on band music in the grounds. The exhibition was intended to inaugurate the new museum and art gallery built in Kelvingrove, below, and paid for with the profits of the first International Exhibition held on the site in 1888.

The main façade and entrance of Glasgow Art Gallery & Museum on Argyle Street, above, in the early 1900s. The idea for a new gallery came from the Association for the Promotion of Art and Music whose architectural competition was won by Sir J.W. Simpson and Milner Allen in 1892. The adjudicator was Sir Alfred Waterhouse, architect of the Natural History Museum in London, and many blame him for the riotous design that was chosen for Kelvingrove. When money ran out Glasgow Corporation completed the building. The exhibition and art gallery were opened together on 2 May 1901 by the Duke and Duchess of Fife, Princess Louise, eldest daughter of Edward VII. Below is the interior of the central hall with the electric organ which was transferred from the Grand Concert Hall demolished after the close of the Exhibition.

The central hall of the art gallery and museum in the early 1900s, looking towards the main entrance, was designed to display sculpture and featured rather striking art nouveau brass electric light fittings. The whole building was fireproof, built of brick with a vaulted concrete roof, using red Dumfriesshire sandstone outside and blond Giffnock sandstone inside. The halls and corridors were paved with marbles from Norway, Belgium and Italy and the galleries floored in rich woods. A separate competition took place to provide sculptures to adorn the exterior walls and roofs. No wonder the eventual cost was a well over-budget £257,000. The exhibition closed on 9 November 1901 having admitted up to 13 million people, many of whom also trooped through the new art gallery and museum.

The next great event at Kelvingrove, the Scottish Exhibition of Natural History, Art and Industry, took place in 1911. It was a showcase for Scottish history, culture and enterprise, and profits were used to endow a Chair of Scottish History and Literature at Glasgow University.

The Palace of History was the 1911 Exhibition's main building and was modelled on the royal palace of Falkland with elements of Holyrood thrown in. It was built around what remained of Kelvingrove mansion and housed the most comprehensive collection of historic Scottish paintings and artefacts ever assembled. Items were borrowed from 1,400 owners and collectively insured for a massive £459,000.

A band performing in the arcaded Music Court attached to the Palace of Industry. At first-floor level Miss Cranston's Red Lion lunch and tea rooms provided plentiful refreshment to the weary exhibition-goers, who were able to relax to the sounds of the large musical offering below. At night the courtyard was lit up with fairy lights and described as a 'dream of beauty'. The main building here, behind the stage, is the exhibition administrative block and conference hall.

The key image of the exhibition was the Tower of the Palace of Industry, although the industrial displays were less prominent than they had been in the 1901 Exhibition and there were fewer exhibitors. Science and electrical engineering were regarded much more favourably, perhaps reflecting the relative decline of heavy engineering in the wider Glasgow economy.

Despite the worthy educational aims of the 1911 Exhibition, it was realised that success depended on music and popular entertainments for mass appeal. A large area on the north side of Kelvingrove Park was set aside for 'amusements' on an unprecedented scale. The centre of attention here is the Whirlpool ride and to

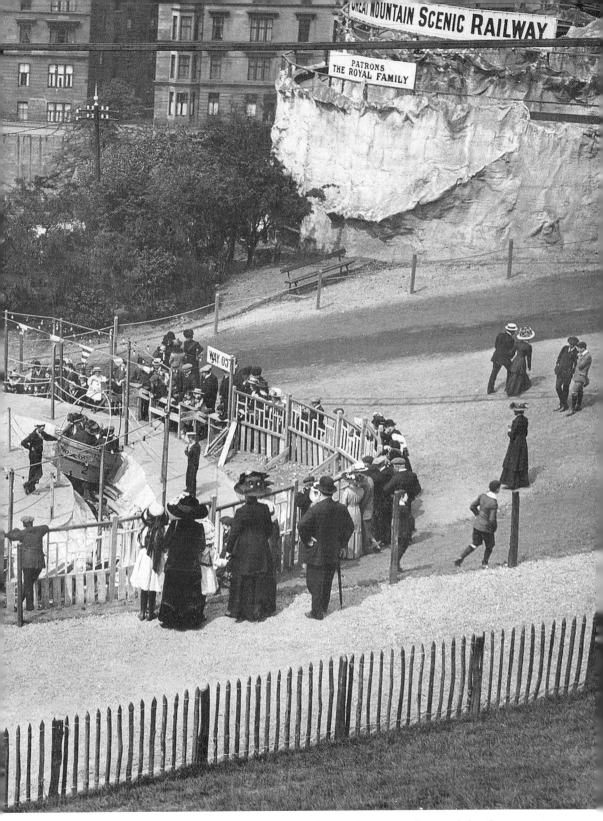

the right is the mile-long Great Mountain Scenic Railway advertising the royal family as patrons. Restaurants and refreshment rooms were dotted around the park and provided by the Glasgow firms of Miss Cranston, McKillop & Sons and, here, W. & R.S. Kerr's Carlton Restaurant, Luncheon and Tea Rooms.

The Great Mountain Scenic Railway certainly looks a little bumpy but mountainous it wasn't. Part of the scenery included a flimsy-looking temporary windmill. This state-of-the-art ride was brought from White City in London. In the centre is another attraction – the Mysterious River Ride – offering 'romance for youths and maidens'.

Crowds attending an open-air performance (probably band music) in the main exhibition venue, the Grand Amphitheatre, seen from the balcony of McKillop & Son's Grosvenor restaurant. On the left is the Garden Club (privileged membership two guineas) which had its own refreshment facilities, with Miss Cranston's White Cockade restaurant on the right.

The organisers of the 1911 Exhibition created a convincing new town full of amazing sights and buildings. On the left is the Palace of History looking towards the tower of the Concert Hall and roofs of the restaurant and Kelvin Hall. On the right is one of the many kiosks scattered around the site and selling all manner of goods, in this case fruit purveyed by Malcolm Campbell. It is hard to believe that all these buildings were temporary structures made of wood, asbestos panels, plaster, cement and the judicious use of steel frames, all with a generous coating of paint. They survived the duration of the exhibition well, helped by the generally favourable weather. There were only twelve unfavourable days, including the wet opening day and stormy final night, during the five months it was open. In total 9,369,375 people attended the exhibition.

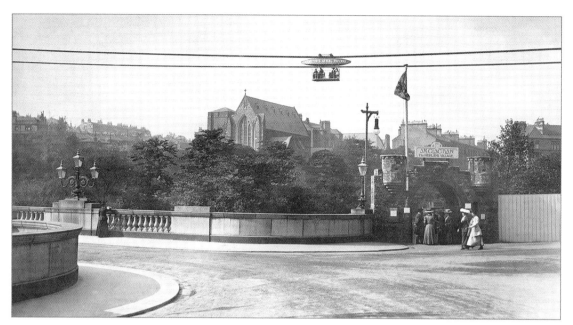

Beside the Prince of Wales Bridge in Kelvingrove Park was the entrance to An Clachan, the Highland village, part of the growing interest in Scottish history and Gaelic culture. Above the River Kelvin a handful of intrepid visitors are taking a ride on the electrically-powered Aerial Railway, invented by W.L. Hamilton of Glasgow, which rose 130 feet to give an impressive view of the whole exhibition site.

The Weaver's Cottage was one of many realistically modelled buildings collectively covering the 3 acres of An Clachan and partly made of plaster fashioned to look like stone walls. It contained a working hand loom used to card and spin wool. Nearby was a supposed smuggler's den with an illicit still, although it was kept uncharacteristically dry of whisky.

An Clachan was a commercial venture which charged admission and sold refreshments and a range of Highland products. The profits were destined for the Co-operative Council of Highland Home Industries. The staff were all Gaelic-speaking highlanders dressed in appropriate costumes, as here in front of the village smithy. On the right are bundles of withies used to make the basketware sold to visitors.

The design of the post office building was based on the traditional Highland black house. It was also operated as a Gaelic bookshop by Alexander McLaren & Son of Argyle Street, Glasgow. An Clachan was a popular attraction and, apart from its immediate commercial goals, aimed to educate people about Gaelic language and culture.

Dancers and musicians were part of the 100-strong community of West Africans and Sudanese who made up the African Village in the 'entertainment' part of the exhibition. Nearby was the Arctic Village, below, populated by Laplanders. What they made of the inquisitive alien sightseers is not known, nor is it recorded what happened to them after the end of the exhibition. Their reindeer, however, ended up in Regent's Park Zoo, London. Some felt it demeaning to make such a spectacle of 'primitive' fellow human beings, but they were undoubtedly a popular draw.

The Highland village complemented the 'Olde Toun' on the main exhibition site, which recreated elements of old burgh architecture populated by costumed olde-world inhabitants. Behind the couple on the left is the shop of T.R. Annan & Sons of Sauchiehall Street, the official exhibition photographers, who also took this view.

West of Kelvingrove lies the Western Infirmary, on Dumbarton Road and Church Street, seen here before the First World War. It was built as the teaching hospital for Glasgow University's medical school and to provide for the growing population west of the city centre. It was opened in 1874. Over the years parts of it have been demolished and extensions added in the interests of modernisation. Its excellent service continues.

ACKNOWLEDGEMENTS

The photographs and associated information in this volume have been obtained from a variety of sources too numerous to list, although I am particularly grateful to John MacKenzie for his help, information and encouragement. I must also thank the staff of the Mitchell Library, Glasgow, and of Glasgow Museums for aiding the historical research required and helping to trace photograph copyright owners where they have remained elusive.

The Library of the University of St Andrews has kindly extended permission to reproduce images in my own collection which were originated by the famed postcard publishers, James Valentine & Sons of Dundee, found on pages 44 (lower) and 66 (lower); and Scottish Power for the photograph on page 32 (lower). Apologies to the small number of photographers or copyright holders I have been unable to trace. Finally, I must be thankful for Glasgow origins on my father's side – could anybody wish for more?